MW00624160

The ABC's OF Niceness

ACKNOWLEDGEMENT

When I decided to put my thoughts into a "guidebook" for creating more "niceness" in our world, I knew that the person to illustrate my book was Bob Cargill, a quintessential artist and long-time dear friend. He listened patiently and then took my ideas and developed the way to present them in engaging and expressive illustrations for the reader. He has made this book what I wanted it to be.

My gratitude also to my son, Alex, who actually listened when I taught the ABC's of niceness and character to him as a child; my daughter-in-law, Annabel; my brothers, Wade and Paul; and a number of friends and co-workers who read the book as it evolved and encouraged me. They believe too that our world needs nice people more and more each day.

And, finally, my appreciation to Barton Wood, the production administrator, whose artistic and coordination talent made this book come together.

DEDICATION

This book is dedicated to my wonderfully responsible parents who instilled in their three children the essential importance of character – attributes of integrity, kindness, gratefulness, honesty, sharing, and, yes, niceness! And also I dedicate this book to my grandson, Finn, in hopes that he will always know the importance of being NICE.

Linda Bleep

B. CARUM

CHARACTER FOR KIDS

There are people in the world who do many good things. But, there are also some people who do bad things. Maybe you know about a playmate who was knocked off his or her bicycle by another child. Maybe someone said something mean to you or your friend. You might be sad when you hear that. You might wonder why someone would do a bad thing. You might be thinking: "Why can't people be nice to each other so everybody in the world can be happy?"

You might also be thinking: "Can I do something to help people in the world be nicer to each other?"

This book is written to explain to you how you can make the world better. So – if YOU do something nice for somebody, and that person does something

nice for someone else, and that person does something nice for another person, little by little the world can become a happier place for everybody. Isn't that a good idea?!

So the good news is that there are many ways YOU can make the world nicer. This book gives you 26 ways. Why 26? Because that is the number of letters in the alphabet, and that makes it easy to remember each word.

In the back of this book is a page of "STARS". Every time you show someone – your parents, grandparents, teachers, or other adults – that you are doing something to make the world a nicer place, they can put a GOLD STAR* on the page in this book that is one of the 26 ways you are doing your part. When the pages are full of gold stars, you know you are well on your way to becoming the kind of person the world needs!

Just think – if YOU do 26 things, and your friends do those 26 things too, how much nicer the world will be!

Now
are YOU ready? Let's begin...

You know that there are rules in life

That people must obey.

Don't cross the street when cars go by;

Do what your parents say.

Please make your bed; take out the trash;

Go to bed when you are told.

Study hard; don't lie or cheat;

Then you'll deserve a star of gold!

ABIDE BY RULES

Believe in yourself in all you do,

Know you can do whatever you decide to;

Learn to ride a bike or paint, or even write a song –

Yes, goals are good for YOU.

When you work hard, with confidence

You can achieve goals and be proud;

You should always do your best, who knows –

You may stand out in the crowd!

BELIEVE IN YOURSELF

Being courteous is always nice,

It shows respect for those you meet;

Don't interrupt; say "ma'am" and "sir",

Courtesies are very neat.

Remember to say "excuse me" and "please",

And "thanks", to be polite;

Then others want to be nice to you –

Such courtesies are always right.

BE **COURTEOUS**

Being dependable is simply doing

What you say that you will do.

And it also is not doing what you say

That you won't do;

When you can be depended on

For what you do and say,

Then you are called reliable

And that is the best way.

BE **DEPENDABLE**

Show enthusiasm about what you have today –

Your family and friends, your school and time to play;

Be interested in your schoolwork,

And in what your teachers have to say.

Enthusiasm is the "oomph" that helps you to succeed;

When studying for a spelling bee

Or learning how to play at sports,

Being excited is the way to be!

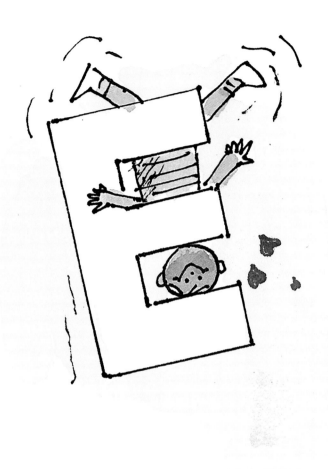

BE ENTHUSIASTIC

Sometimes when you play in sports

Or take a test in school,

You finish last in grade or score,

And that is not too "cool".

So when you finish low or last,

There's no need to worry or whine

Try harder; study more; don't cry;

Next time you may be first in line.

FINISH BEST

To be grateful is to be thankful for

The goodness in your life each day;

Your mom, dad, sister, brother, friend

All love you in their special way.

Be grateful for your family and home

And school, to learn new things.

For your computer, doll, or basketball –

Don't forget to count your blessings!

BE **GRATEFUL**

How many times have people been helpful to you?

Carrying a backpack or tying your shoes?

Or helping you with homework

When answers seemed to have no clues?

You too can be helpful to others

With a smile on your face every day;

You can make things better or easy,

It will make you feel good, don't you say?

BE **HELPFUL**

Integrity is a big word, for sure;

It has a big meaning for you.

When you are said to have integrity,

You are honest and sincere and true.

You think about others,

You want to do right;

You always are caring,

So your future is bright!

HAVE **INTEGRITY**

Happiness comes with a game or a toy,

It may last an hour, a week, or a day;

But joyfulness is a feeling you carry inside

No matter what happens, it stays.

When you're joyful, you think of all people,

You don't cry or argue or pout;

Joy can't be taken by others

When you show "sunshine" within and without!

BE **JOYFUL**

Kindness is a quality that focuses on others,

Doing nice things for someone as such

Will make them feel happy and trusting again

And will give you a happiness rush.

So when you do kind things for others

For parent, brother, cousin, or friend,

YOU become the lucky one, it's true –

The payback to you has no end.

BE **KIND**

This may seem like an interesting word –

Suggesting when you laugh you seem nice?

Because some people will laugh at others,

Making fun of their speaking and dress.

Laughing <u>at</u> someone is wrong and so sad,

But sharing a laugh that hurts none

Is a great way to be close to all of your friends

And have a good time with much fun.

LAUGH

Have manners at the table

When you're eating every meal;

Don't eat your food with fingers,

No matter how you feel.

Cut your meat; don't slurp your soup;

Your elbows off the table;

Manners show respect for self

And others when you're able.

HAVE **MANNERS**

What does it mean to be nice to others?

It means always saying words that are kind,

Defending a classmate who is bullied,

And keeping good thoughts in your mind.

You know how good it makes you feel

When someone is nice to you –

Well, that is how a friend will feel

When nice things for them you do!

BE **NICE**

Adults may ask you to do some things

You may not want to do;

But they just want you to obey –

You ask "Why?" Here's the clue:

When you obey what you are told

To do or not to do,

It means that you respect

The very ones who care for YOU.

BE **OBEDIENT**

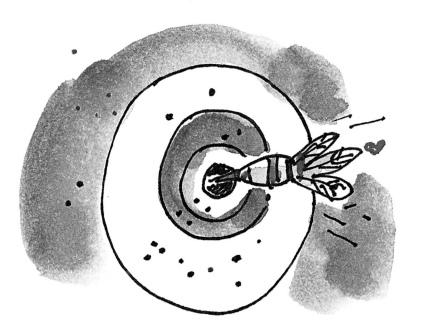

If little brother breaks your favorite game

It's difficult to smile;

But just remember – he feels badly too,

So be patient all the while.

It's hard to always be patient

When people are late or don't listen to you.

But if you show patience and kindness to them,

They just may show patience with you!

BE **PATIENT**

Do you sometimes say, "I wonder why"...

The stars stay in the sky?

Or wonder why your hair is brown

Or why a ball can bounce so high?

When you ask questions, that's how you learn,

And that is very smart;

The world is better when people ask –

It shows you have both brains and heart.

BE **QUESTIONING**

Always show respect for your parents,

They love and want the best for you;

Don't call them names or say bad words,

That's wrong for you to do.

Give respect for family, teachers, and friends,

And, for sure, they'll respect you, too;

It's simply what people can do for each other –

And the world will be nicer, like YOU!

RESPECT OTHERS

When your parent says, "share",

You should share your cookies and toys,

Maybe a video game or a book,

It is right both for girls and for boys.

You like it when someone shares something with you;

When YOU share, you make others feel good;

And when you give time, you give of yourself;

Such sharing benefits all, as it should!

SHARE

When you tell a lie it can "snowball" a lot

And someone's feelings will likely be hurt;

A texted untruth,what you write or you say

Can make someone feel sad with such "dirt'.

So telling the truth is the right thing to do;

It is what everyone knows is the best.

You want others to tell only truth about you

So you need to say truths to the rest.

BE **TRUTHFUL**

As an understanding person you're special

Because for others you care;

You think of yourself in another one's shoes

And friends' problems you offer to share.

Always be willing to consider what others

Are dealing with and why they are sad;

It may be a difficult problem or day,

So your understanding may make someone glad.

BE **UNDERSTANDING**

Do you know what it means to "have values"?

It's an important trait for us all –

It means that you always are fair;

Good character will make you stand tall.

You will be honest and kind and always try

To help your family and friends;

You won't say hurtful things, and

If needed, make amends.

HAVE **VALUES**

When you have a job to be done

Whether school work or chores in your home,

Work hard in how you do your task,

It will be right for reaching your goal.

"Hard working" is a description of character;

For people who do their work well are vital;

They make for a world where much is achieved

Whether gaining praise or awards, or a title.

HAVE **WORK** ETHIC

Always do your school work or task

With the most diligent effort you can;

Not just because it's a good thing to do,

But because it's the very best plan.

When you always try for eXcellence

It says you want to achieve so high;

You're willing to practice and study a lot,

You'll feel pride for your work, no lie!

SEEK EXCELLENCE

Always do what is right for YOU,

In dress or words or actions or looks;

Don't just follow what someone else does –

Everybody must write their own "book".

Just be yourself, and independent in mind,

Think before actions you do;

When you do what is right and not wrong,

To yourself you are happily true.

BE **YOURSELF**

Isn't it great to be alive

To learn new things and play?

To sing and jump and read a book

And make a craft your way?

A zest for life means you have fun;

You study, and jokes you may tell.

You are excited each day when you awake

To know the new day will be well!

HAVE A **ZEST** FOR LIFE

REMEMBER —
IT'S NICE
TO BE IMPORTANT,
BUT IT IS MORE
IMPORTANT TO BE
Nice